W9-AJO-582

Maps

by Wiley Blevins

Reading Consultant: Wiley Blevins, M.A.
Phonics/Early Reading Specialist

 COMPASS POINT BOOKS

Minneapolis, Minnesota

Compass Point Books
3109 West 50th Street, #115
Minneapolis, MN 55410

Visit Compass Point Books on the Internet at *www.compasspointbooks.com*
or e-mail your request to *custserv@compasspointbooks.com*

Photographs ©: Cover and p. 1: DigitalVision, p. 6: Steve Skjold Photography,
p. 11 inset: PhotoDisc/Scenics of America

Editorial Development: Alice Dickstein, Alice Boynton
Photo Researcher: Wanda Winch
Design/Page Production: Silver Editions, Inc.
Illustrator: Angela Gahler

Library of Congress Cataloging-in-Publication Data
Blevins, Wiley.
  Maps / by Wiley Blevins.
      p. cm. — (Compass Point phonics readers)
  Summary: Simply describes how to use a map in easy-to-read text that
  incorporates phonics instruction.
  Includes bibliographical references and index.
    ISBN 0-7565-0512-7 (alk. paper)
   1. Cartography—Juvenile literature. 2. Reading—Phonetic
  method—Juvenile literature. [1. Maps. 2. Reading—Phonetic method.]
  I. Title. II. Series.
    GA105.6.B54 2004
    912'.01'4—dc21   2003006356

Table of Contents

Parent Letter **4**

"The Cock Crows" **5**

Maps **6**

Word List **13**

Nice Going! **14**

Read More **16**

Index **16**

Dear Parent or Caregiver,

Welcome to Compass Point Phonics Readers, books of information for young children. Each book concentrates on specific phonic sounds and words commonly found in beginning reading materials. Featuring eye-catching photographs, every book explores a single science or social studies concept that is sure to grab a child's interest.

So snuggle up with your child, and let's begin. Start by reading aloud the Mother Goose nursery rhyme on the next page. As you read, stress the words in dark type. These are the words that contain the phonic sounds featured in this book. After several readings, pause before the rhyming words, and let your child chime in.

Now let's read *Maps*. If your child is a beginning reader, have him or her first read it silently. Then ask your child to read it aloud. For children who are not yet reading, read the book aloud as you run your finger under the words. Ask your child to imitate, or "echo," what he or she has just heard.

Discussing the book's content with your child:
Explain to your child that on page 10 Alaska and Hawaii are pictured as they are because they are not on the U.S. mainland. After reading page 12, have your child locate the places shown on the map and discuss the routes he or she might take to get from one particular place to another.

At the back of the book is a fun Nice Going! game. Your child will take pride in demonstrating his or her mastery of the phonic sounds and the high-frequency words.

Enjoy Compass Point Phonics Readers and watch your child read and learn!

4

The Cock Crows

The cock **crows** in the morn
To tell us to **rise,**
And **he** that **lies late**
Will never **be wise;**

For early to bed
and early to **rise,**
Is the **way** to **be** healthy
And wealthy and **wise.**

This map is a flat drawing.
It shows us where places are.
It shows us how to get to places.

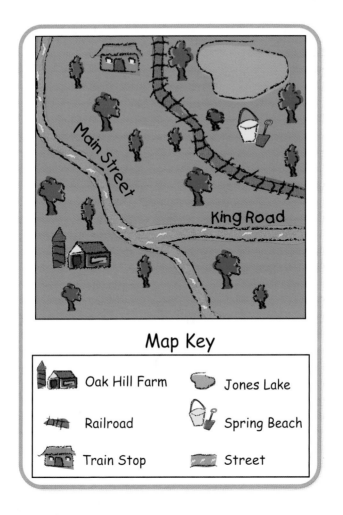

Map Key

Oak Hill Farm		Jones Lake	
Railroad		Spring Beach	
Train Stop		Street	

Maps use symbols.

Symbols are little drawings.

The 🫐 stands for a lake.

The ▰ stands for a street.

A map has directions on it.
We use the directions to read
the map.
The compass rose helps us.

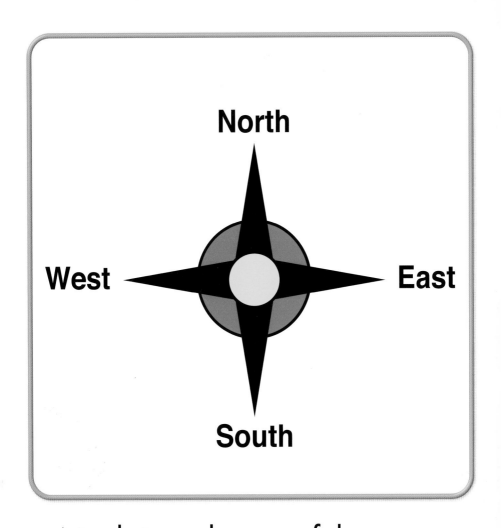

North is at the top of the map.
South is on the bottom.
East is on the right of the map.
West is on the left.

Maps can show a lot of places.
A map can show a town or a state.
This map shows the U.S.A.

A map can't show the real size of a place.

Miami Beach is a big city.

But on the map, it is just a dot.

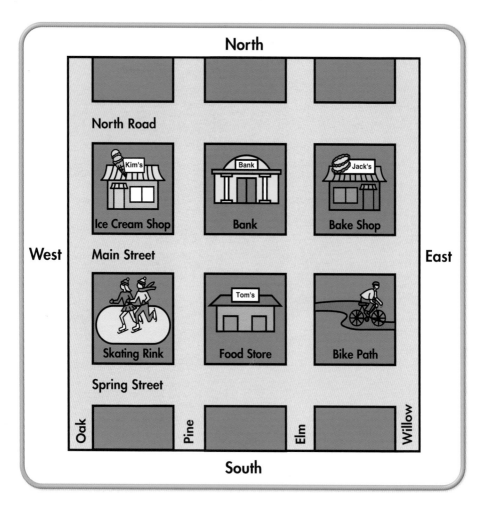

You will need a map some day.
Finding places on a map can
be fun.
What can you find on this map?

Word List

Review of Long Vowels

-ing
finding
skating

High-Frequency
drawing(s)
little

Social Studies
directions
Miami Beach, Florida
North
South
symbols

Nice Going!

Player 1

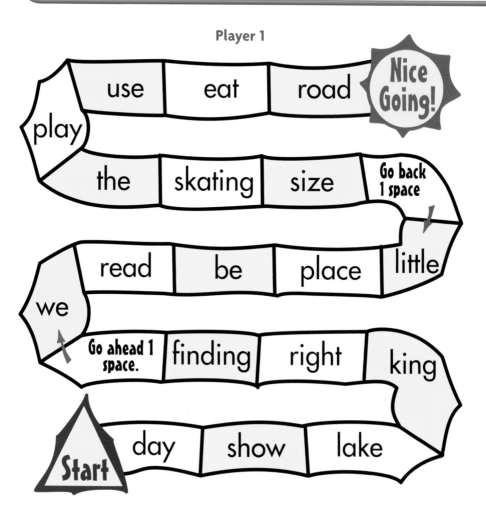

use | eat | road | **Nice Going!**

play

the | skating | size | **Go back 1 space**

read | be | place | little

we

Go ahead 1 space. | finding | right | king

Start | day | show | lake

14

How to Play

- Each player puts a moving piece on his or her Start. Players take turns shaking the penny and dropping it on the table. Heads means move 1 space. Tails means move 2 spaces.
- The player moves and reads the word in the space. If the child cannot read the word, tell him or her what it is. On the next turn, the child must read the word before moving.
- If a player lands on a space having special directions, he or she should move accordingly.
- The first player to reach the *Nice Going!* sign wins the game.

Player 2

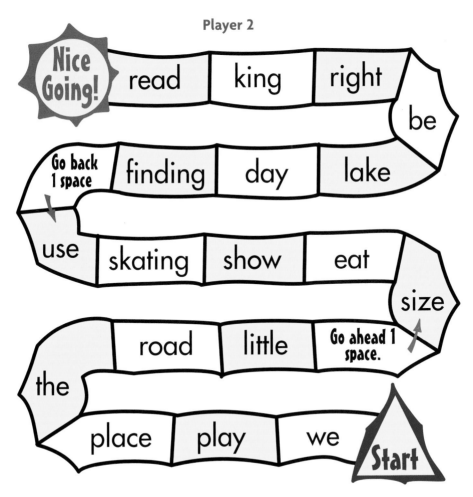

Read More

Aberg, Rebecca. *Map Keys.* Rookie Read-About Geography Series. New York: Children's Press, 2003.

Scott, Janine. *Mapping Our World.* Minneapolis, Minn.: Compass Point Books, 2003.

Wade, Mary Dodson. *Types of Maps.* Rookie Read-About Geography Series. New York: Children's Press, 2003.

Weidenman, Lauren. *What Is a Map?* Mankato, Minn.: Yellow Umbrella Books, 2000.

Index

city, 11

compass rose, 8

directions, 8

drawing(s), 6, 7

lake, 7

Miami Beach, 11

place(s), 6, 10, 11, 12

state, 10

street, 7

symbols, 7

U.S.A., 10